THOMAS HARDY

There were completed in the month of January, nineteen hundred and twenty-nine, by the Pynson Printers of New York, 761 copies of this book of which 550 are to be distributed in America through Random House, each copy signed by the author, this being number

H. M. Tomlinson

THOMAS HARDY

H · M · TOMLINSON

HASKELL HOUSE PUBLISHERS Ltd.

Publishers of Scarce Scholarly Books

NEW YORK, N. Y. 10012

1971

First Published 1929

HASKELL HOUSE PUBLISHERS Ltd.
Publishers of Scarce Scholarly Books
280 LAFAYETTE STREET
NEW YORK, N. Y. 10012

Library of Congress Catalog Card Number: 70-160129

Standard Book Number 8383-1283-7

Printed in the United States of America

THOMAS HARDY

IT was January 12, 1928, and a winter sunrise that gave my empty suburban street an unrecognisable look of splendour. I think the chimneys of our houses were of gold, and the walls and roofs of jasper and amethyst, which is nothing like them. That glowing and unfamiliar vista was as if I had surprised a secret celebration of the earth and sky; we were not supposed to see it; it was to fade into our own place before we were about. As I looked out on my changed street I was repeating the haunting thought of the night: "Hardy is dead." But the knowledge that our own light had gone out accorded with the colours of that high dawn. We so often associate a thought of Hardy with the aspect of the earth and sky. The heavens and the earth were always the chief characters in the dramas of that poet; over mere mortals presided the eternal sky and the shadowy presence of the earth. So it seemed right for the street to be empty, and to be strange with a transfiguring glow. Hardy had gone.

Within an hour, as the sunrise foretold, came the wind and rain. Roofs and sky turned to lead. The spurts of rain thickened the glass of my window. There was going to be time enough indoors to think about Hardy, yet to think to little purpose; not really to think, but to stare unseeing at the sullen clouds and the rain, for beyond them was a dream world more vivid and stable than the elements, a visionary country in which one had strayed in the reading of nearly forty years, and there had watched Destiny compelling men and women who were more real than one's neighbours— even though one judged Destiny itself was often too conscious of its job to be real; and to remember the venerable little man, whose magic had established that sublimation of the real and changing world, as we saw him at Max Gate shortly before his fatal illness began, sitting with the flames of a log-fire reflecting in his quick eyes, while he talked blithely of poetry, speculated on the prehistoric earthworks to be seen from his house, and smiled at the gossip of the town.

But though there was all day to think about him, there was no likelihood of making a contribution to wisdom, no chance of a critical adjustment which would help to place the poet's urn with precision. For we cannot be dispassionate now. We cannot stand apart from our personal feelings, and so we cannot be critics, for in criticism, as we know, we ought to do what no man has ever done; we ought to consider the work of a poet apart from changeable human opinions, and see it simply as an isolated work of art, bereaved of kinship. Luckily for Hardy's contemporaries they are not called upon to be critics who will be strictly just to him by all those fundamental laws of art which yet somehow include, when we wish them to, any curious departure from precedent. It is not for us to attempt impartial justice, but only to exalt him or otherwise—explain his sublimity or his want of taste—as the moods vary, and this thing of his, or that, is consonant or not with the way we ourselves would have handled the matter; though certainly, as to one characteristic of the poet, most of us will agree. We cannot but observe, and with profound regret, Hardy's brooding sorrow over the ways of humanity. We have to question that oddity. How could so great a mind, in the face of our handsome progress, declare the unhappiness of our state? But it is not our business now to prove the poet's life-long error by pointing to those agreeable steps heavenward in the late history of humanity which joyfully mock the sad and compassionate poet.

Today we must have differing views of Hardy, but it cannot be helped. Instinctively we shall separate, for we know what we want, the beauty of his work, which we desire, from the truth in it, which not seldom is undesirable. Hardy cannot succeed where Jesus failed. That truth and beauty are strangely one need not concern those who prefer the simple method of separating what is comforting in a book from what is challenging and disturbing. We find it difficult to admit that a poet's thought may be beautiful because of its contrast with the darkness of our customary ways, for that would mean that beauty convicted us. It is not the business of poetry to do that. Poetry is an irrelevant solace at leisure, which is pleasant, as is wine, after the dustiness of a harsh and insistent world. Besides, its ideas may be contrary to revealed religion, and a poet is not a prophet. We do not desire that he should give us Revelations. No apocalypse for us, if you please. So it need not surprise us that one of our most paradoxical and confident essayists— to whom good and evil are difficulties no longer, but are easily separated because his Church provides him with an infallible test—when his opinion was sought by an interviewer on the news of the death of the poet, said of the author of *The Dynasts* that Hardy was a "nice courteous gentleman, rather simple minded." Which is quite right, as far as it goes, and indeed shows less intolerance than dismissing Hardy merely as the village atheist blaspheming over the village idiot; though the essayist's commendation is applicable to so many people, fortunately, that it seems hardly worth space in a newspaper to record virtues so usual. Then again, the London daily papers, by their various placards on the morning after Thomas Hardy's death, betrayed the fact that not every one of them was prepared on the instant to estimate the importance of the news.

Some of them did not consider his passing to be more important than some other subjects, which surprise compelled us to note. One paper was anxious that we should "Read our new serial: 'Frail Wives'." Another asked: "Who will give Jix £100,000?" The contents bill of another famous London daily paper bore simply the cryptic numerals "1857428"; though whether those figures referred to a successful feat of circulation, or were indeed a cabalistic advertisement of a fatal conjunction of numbers which made inevitable the passing of a great man, it was impossible for a non-reader to guess. Yet another of our daily papers placarded an outburst entitled: "Ambassadors Cars." That may have been a special edition devoted to automobiles of luxury, but I cannot say, for I did not buy the paper. And later in the day one afternoon paper of the capital of the British Empire, a paper once famous for its liberal outlook on the world, gave a bare half-column to the news that the greatest figure in European literature, who happened to be English, had died, apparently because its editorial staff was too astonished by Mrs. Snyder's New Lease of Life. There were other periodicals, however, which did make the appropriate comment and whose estimates of the significance of the principal news of the day were serious; yet these little things show us that the stress of the exciting nature of the living day, its fears, dog-fights, rumours, executions, crime, and market prices, tend to confuse our sense of the value of what is lovely and of good report. It is not easy to turn from the attraction of what draws our attention to the estimate of the worth of a creator of beauty. Beauty, if it be there, will last longer than the interesting things about us; but that does not mean much to those who cannot see it. Said a London Councillor once, in the peroration of his speech which demanded the destruction of London's finest bridge, "as for its beauty, I have never seen it." Yes, but he failed to see also that the very horses which plod over it daily are in the same cart with him.

Some of us are old enough to remember the violence of the attacks on Hardy and his morality when his last novels appeared. And beyond his immorality he made plain his vulgarity; his taste was liable to deplorable lapses. But though that reception of his later novels helped to decide him against writing any more prose for us, yet when I met him first, and this was referred to, he was reluctant to look back at it, though presently, when he saw I could recall the controversies in some detail, he did begin to gossip of that phase of his past, but in so low and tolerant a tone that you might have thought he never had any feeling about it. Once I began to move uneasily at his recital of the course of one

xii

outrageous attack, but Hardy's face did not lose its good humour, nor his voice its gentleness. He was only talking of criticism in the abstract, and this was part of the evidence. I should doubt that Hardy was ever made angry, except by cruelty to the lowly and unimportant. He was a great man, if a sign of that is simplicity and modesty so surprising that they might be childish innocence. It was a shock to talented visitors to find, when they met him, that the man who wrote *The Woodlanders* and *The Return of the Native* seemed not so clever as they. A meeting with Hardy was comforting to self-esteem. He was venerable, he was indeed already a legend; his great epic which placed him next to Shakespeare was published over twenty years ago; yet all that seemed rather odd, too, because the little old man himself, as he entertained us, might have been the youngest and most innocent of us all. He appeared content to talk of the habits of owls, and of the signs of the weather, of local inns and queer characters, and of the strangeness of hearing in Dorchester by wireless telephony the dancers' feet when an orchestra was playing at a London festival. Trivial life interested him. Little things amused him. Little things, you could see, often had for him a significance which a clever listener failed to grasp. Hardy was a simple man. A meeting with Hardy made it possible to understand why those very clever men about Shakespeare left for us such scant testimony of the fellow who wrote *Anthony and Cleopatra*. That fellow of the Sonnets was a smiling and good-natured man, we must suppose, who was so simple there was little to say about him. He never made unkind epigrams, it was not easy to quarrel with him, and he did not get excited, not even when the Armada was scattered. Now and then, perhaps, he would drop an odd remark from his corner of the tavern, which made listeners stare, and wonder what he meant. There seemed nothing but queerness in it, until later, when the phrase was remembered because of an awkward coincidence in life. Then it became explicable, in a new light. Mere chance, though, that thought of his. It was the experience which brought the light. Shakespeare had spoken more wisely than he knew.

Hardy, too, had so innocent a divination into people and their motives that sometimes when talking to him you felt this child was as old as humanity and knew all about us, but that he did not attach importance to his knowledge because he did not know he had it. Just by chance, in the drift of the talk, there would be a word by Hardy, not only wide of the mark, but apparently not directed to it. Why did he say it? On the way home, or some weeks later, his comment would be recalled, and with the revealing light on it.

Max Gate is a walled little island of trees on the road to Egdon Heath, just outside Dorchester. No house can be seen from the road. I fancy Hardy planted most of that screen of leaves. It suggests the hiding place of a recluse. There is an approach across the fields from the town, and in summer that was the way to go, with Came Hill lifting darkly beyond a sea of corn, and the isolated promontory sculptured by men long before the Romans landed, now called Maiden Castle, in the distance. The square tower of Fordington Church and the chimneys of the town floated near on the tree-tops of a hollow. You felt sure you would find Hardy in that country, even though the footpath was uncertain. It looked like his country. But it had fallen dusk in sharp winter weather when we were there last. In fact, it was the month before he died. The house then was only a lantern in a dim porch. A spray of cotoneaster had left the mass of shadow to get into the light of the lantern; it was the only sign of a wall.

Mrs. Hardy always knew how to keep out intrusions such as easterly winds. Her house was as warm and comforting that evening as a quiet heart. The old man, brisk and youthful, showed us where we should sit to get the benefit of the fire. There was a lazy smoke-coloured Persian cat—appropriately named Cobweb--who stretched and yawned, and was an assurance of the ease and rightness of the time and place. It was certainly the fireside to get to the heart of the matter, though leisurely. If our talk gave out, then there were the reflections of the lively fire playing on the face of the old poet, who contemplated the bright logs, his eyebrows raised, his legs stretched out, his hands between his knees. That seamed face lost sight of the visitors for a while, and its nervous interest in the gossip changed to the compassionate look of a man who had brooded for long on the world, but was not sure he had made out what it all meant, or could do it the good he desired for it. It may be true that as a man thinks so is he, and that may be why Hardy's head was satisfying with expected beauty. Some who met him say that you would not have known Hardy for a poet. Perhaps that is because the younger poets frequent the town, and are so often seen and heard. We get to think that a poet should resemble the pattern of a poet. Hardy did not. He resembled in no particular way any other poet you may have met. He might have been a retired solicitor of the country town, pursuing keenly in his leisure several hobbies, finding cheerful entertainment in the fact that his house was on the side of a patrician graveyard of the Romans, and that when gardening he sometimes turned up relics; that there were signs nearby that men unknown had a grove to their god long before Cæsar came; startling you with the remark that Robert Louis Stevenson, when he saw him last, was sitting in your chair; admitting strangely then, for a man of his years, that he read poetry nowadays and very little prose, but that he enjoyed the prose of Sir Thomas Browne and Lamb, and preferred Sterne to Swift. It would not be odd, but quite in keeping, that a retired solicitor should have a shrewder knowledge of men and women than a fashionable novelist. His interests turned quickly with any change of the conversation. He would give you a rum story of a dog, and you had to admit it was stranger than your own anecdote; so very strange indeed that you fell silent, wondering what on earth the clue to the mystery could be.

Yet when Hardy was in repose his face was that of a seer. There was no doubt then, no need to wonder what special privilege had admitted him to so intimate a knowledge of his fellows. That little man, with wisps of soft grey hair resting on the collar of his tweed jacket, for his hair would grow long at the back; blue-eyed, with a masterful nose that turned slightly from the straight, whose raised and questioning eyebrows pushed furrows up his forehead to the bald and shapely head, had with his life work taken the place in English literature next to Shakespeare; and it was always easy for me to feel that there was the very man. What those people were told who asked for signs and wonders, we know. There the wonder was. There sat the author of *The Dynasts*. And here, while we are at Max Gate, is where we should acknowledge the debt we owe to Mrs. Hardy, for she ordained that he should be with us longer than his frailty otherwise would have allowed.

While Hardy was with us his presence gave dignity to our day. He was English, but because he was the embodiment of qualities which are essentially of the tradition, and because he belonged to the land as much as the heath and hawthorns of Egdon, and the dateless barrows on the hill tops about his home, and the stones of his village church, he represented us in a way that Parliament cannot, and so he belongs to those in every country who judge their neighbours by the best their neighbours have done. There is more of the salt of English life in the talk of the characters who move in Hardy's novels, and more of the English land in his scenes, than in all Hansard, and in all the controversies and guide-books. If strangers wish to know us, let them read Hardy; but then, they will see only themselves in his poems and stories. Hodge over his beer in a Dorset inn, even when his drink has been aggrieved by politicians and the press, sometimes drops a word which is more convincing than the upshot of a Parliamentary debate. It is not recorded, except in Hardy; and yet perhaps it may be the last word on the subject, though it may take a century or two for it to be repeated with effective emphasis. Such words are like the flints in the soil; they belong to it, and are sure to show when the earth is stirred.

It is likely that if a company of English writers and critics were asked by a foreigner, who did not know us, to what book he could turn for just such a picture of England as would convince a native that it was the origin of his bones, and his nurture, and his destiny, those men might, in the conventional way, consider first an exultant passage from Shakespeare. But I think that if one of them were to mention the opening chapter of *The Return of the Native,* then the others, after a little surprise, would agree. There it is—at least for the Englishman of today—in as memorable a prose passage as there is in the language, that description of Egdon Heath at sunset. And it is not in its sombreness, which might be of the dusk, nor of some fancied impress there of things well done which are forgotten; nor in the vague brightness of the last of the evening light in the sky, a light which might be the casual and accustomed sanction for what then is disappearing below into night; nor in the vague spaciousness of the heath; nor in those grotesque and dilated shadows which familiar objects assume in such a solitude at sundown to a sensitive traveller, shades that could be the nightly peopling of the scene by those who once knew it, but are gone. It is in such apprehensions, but there is something more, too; there is the entirely unreasonable surmise that we knew the heath before that gnarled thorn was young, before that white ribband of road was new to it, before the barrows were on the lonely ridges of the downs. I cannot believe this surmise is of pride in the continuity of the English. It is quite intimate. It has nothing to do with race, though perhaps it is not without a sense of fellowship.

Hardy himself never understood—or so it seemed to me, and, anyhow, I suppose such a modest man would not find it easy to believe it—that the people of his tales and the scenes in which they move are part of the life of the present English world; that the light from the country of his dreams falls across our reality and makes significant and so more easily endurable its garishness. We have forgotten him as a great writer; his creation is part of our traditional landscape. We are to believe, on excellent authority, that we betray our provincialism if, when speaking of novels and novelists, we permit the mention of the more important English writers until after many Russians have been named.

There is, says the voice of authority, a virtue called characterisation, and the Russian novels have it, but the English in but an inferior way. Certainly this sounds difficult or wise. Yet suddenly we remember that there is more characterisation in the last popular novel by a candid young lady than in all Greek drama. Where are we now? There is more particular characterisation in Proust than in all Shakespeare. So what of it? Modern novels are full of characterisation, and, good and bad together, they all soon die. Their candid revelations of character do not save them. So there is a chance, as the story called *Macbeth* still lives on, that we are deceived by what the fashion of the hour declares to be chiefly good in a story. We may as well be called provincial for it as anything else if we decline to displace the author of the Wessex novels. For it may still be true that the earth, and the sky, and the mystery of the force we call life, are more wonder-compelling than the oddities of any character we are likely to meet. The earth was older as a character than Napoleon even when he died, and it seems as though something latent in the earth over-bore him and all his projects, whether or not that force was purposive, whether or not there is an Immanent Will. The earth was here before the earliest of man. What word was given to it? We shall never learn that. Perhaps the earth merely got going. Maybe compassion, which came with man, was as accidental as the plesiosaurus or as falling downstairs. There is no telling. We cannot learn what the word was, if there were a word; yet if you read again the first chapter of *The Woodlanders;* or if on the top of Norcombe Hill with its "ancient and decaying plantation of beeches" you watch with Gabriel Oak while he revives a new born lamb by a fire in his hut, and looks to the stars for the time, to see where the earth has swung to in the heavens, then an apprehension of that which transcends brief mortal life lets fall its shadow over your reading. But the author gives it no name. Not only is there no name for it, but the creator of beauty is unaware of what he does. Nevertheless, a conviction of continuity has come to us through our reading, though the very stars are passing. The conviction, it is true, may be only another of our illusions; yet we need not trouble to prove our conviction, for what was beautiful induced it, and beauty can have no weight in an argument. It is known, but it is beyond our words. Yet is beauty an illusion? That cannot be when, for a bare instant, the ancient riddle seemed on the point of solution. A light from nowhere transfigured, for a moment, our grey and accustomed levels, and though the light is withdrawn its revelation is remembered; as if a dawn out of its appointed order in the years had surprised the place we know, and then instantly went. Hardy can surprise with such intuitions, which, if we are pressed, we freely admit have geographical bearings no more exact than the faery seas forlorn seen from another magic casement. There is something in Hardy which is more than salty rustic talk, and the smell of woodfires and of damp leaves and cider presses, and the look of the autumn earth, which make *The Woodlanders* such comfortable reading. Hardy is all that, and of mornings before sun-up, with lanterns dodging among the waggons, hurdles, and faggots in the yard of the timber merchant of Little Hintock, where we meet Giles Winterbourne, the man who could so plant trees that they always flourished; and he is, too, the capacious old barns of Bathsheba Everdene's farm, where the flocks were shorn, and where the sunlight on ancient walls which had witnessed centuries of such busy scenes, and the pungent fleece, were inseparable from the play of mind between Gabriel Oak and his beautiful but wayward young mistress. And Hardy is the High Street of Casterbridge and its cornchandler, and a multitude of other men and women, and of familiar places so well accustomed to the ways of our fellows, and so unchanged in nature by the passage of time, that we feel those hamlets must be as enduring as the hills around them, and have foundations deeper than the roots of dynasties. There it is. Hardy suggests a ghostly virtue which chance and time cannot touch. Whatever that quality may be which suffuses our common words when a poet uses them, somehow it gives them an unaccustomed authority. The poet uses our common tongue to a new purpose, and we feel that after empires have fallen, still the poet and his people will be there. The next sunrise after the great downfall, the outlasting smoke is seen rising from cottage hearths, and a poet is still guarding the lamp which man once lighted.

Not so fast, though. For since Hardy's death a special correspondent, as newspapers say, has been to Dorchester, and there he made the soothing discovery that Hardy is not read. The *Daily News* representative journeyed all the way from London, and enquired of the young lady at the office desk of his hotel in Casterbridge—a quite natural and easy beginning for him—and without any fuss she admitted it. She cannot read Hardy. He is too sad. A tobacconist of the town agreed with her. They both named the authors they did read, though it is not for me to repeat the famous names. The great daily paper thereupon announced next morning the important discovery in its headlines, "Hardy is too sad," on the word of those local authorities. It must be confessed that the hotel clerk, the tobacconist, and the journalist, expressed a common opinion. I suppose we had better face the fact that now Hardy has gone there will be the usual attempts to diminish the significance of a poet's word to us. He will be too sad, and he will be unlike some other writers, and other things will be wrong with him. The same type of mind, a common type, which never dared to look at the realities of war while they could be seen, nor would hear without a show of impatience the bleak advice of witnesses who knew, are quite willing now to applaud the romantic art of the cinema when it presents that war made vicariously out of dummies, fireworks, and heroics. A test of intelligence, we are told, is an ability to understand the implications of things. It is therefore clear that if we steadily decline to look at the realities of life, when they are painful, then our intelligence will be free from the application of a test so serious. We shall not be found out. There will be no need for us to admit the truth, because we shall not know it. Hardy is too sad: Something else, and it is very important for us, is gained by our refusal to look at a saddening subject. We have escaped from more than one danger. If we deny Hardy, then we are exempt from contrast with a standard which would make us appear to be small. For he is not only sorrowful, he is great. Comparison with the great is unlucky. And if, being wise and great, he should be right, what are we? It is a simple instinct which makes us turn impatiently from the challenge of over-shadowing figures such as Tolstoy and Hardy, and decline to look their way. We do not want to know. It was the work of the same sound instinct in us which took that terrible exposure of human follies, *Gulliver's Travels,* and made of it a gift book for children.

Yes, we can always put these challenging figures in a place where they will not be too noticeable, and we have ways of muffling their words. Their words might make a difference; and we do not want any difference. We prefer to make ourselves comfortable, and the taking of thought would not help. These men are disturbing. A common admission of the truth in their words would shatter so many of our ways and institutions that it is safer, we feel sure, to keep the teacher crucified. We know well, and without reasoning it out, what we are about. We know that a mind which could conceive *War and Peace,* or *The Dynasts,* must be wiser than our own, and must have access to knowledge beyond our range, and so we deny it; or, at the best, accept only so much of it as will not admit anxious criticism into our cheerful and haphazard ways of life. If we look to such men at all, we never fail to secure the satisfaction afforded by their clay feet. Hardy gave us many volumes of verse; and yet, exclaimed a damaging critic recently, it is doubtful whether he wrote more than thirty good poems. No more than thirty? We are constrained to put the humble question: When is a poet not a poet? It might help us to understand the reason for the rarity of poetry if we knew how often the poet must perform the miraculous before we confess the miracle. For we remember that now we do not count the odes of Keats, nor refuse Coleridge because of his fragments. Had we not better be on our guard? It will be always easy for us to find reasons against admitting the light, because we guess at once, when threatened by the danger of illumination, that if darkness should go it would leave much disclosed that was quite well, while it was unseen.

While Hardy lived he justified the least of us, who serve humbly in Athena's temple. His presence did much to re-deem this new age of mechanical science, in which the swarming Barbarians, who never doubt their appetites as men of civility question the difficulties of wisdom or falter at the exactions of art and learning, appear again to have taken control of the destinies of our cities. The Barbarians come this time, not in skins and with crude swords, but armed with the awful powers which engineering and chemi-cal science have given them. We are compelled to submit to the discipline of their bristling tanks, and to the moulding of public opinion in the machinery of the popular news-paper press to the forms of thought which money finds most profitable; and to the reduction of our aspirations to a few simple and standardised desires that can be satisfied easily with public pomps and games, with music by mechanical apparatus, and a criticism of life by cinematograph drama. In such a world a great poet is unique, and definitely alien. His presence is a challenge to its powers. He keeps in heart the lesser men who oppose the things of the mind, though with no apparent success, to both the insolence of authority and the noise of the market place.

It is the rare and isolated figure of the supreme artist which has always justified mankind, and kept hope alive in us; for at times it is hard not to despair over our fellow men, who, with 'loyal luckless hearts," as Hardy shows in *The Dynasts*, suffer our world, built of so much pain and labour, to be snatched at by gamblers to play with, and perhaps to lose, using its continents as boards for the chance of the dice. The poet justifies us because he himself is subli-mated humanity. He embodies and exalts what is best in men and women, and for that very reason his poetry, because it expresses our better self, gives us the illusion that it is not practical. Politics can be practical, but not poetry. Yet we cannot help feeling a doubt that the Beatitudes may be beautifully impossible merely because we prefer the cheerful sensations of the great oratory and great doings by those statesmen and warriors who still set the world by the ears. Those great men are practical men—men of action, as the saying is—and in the wreckage and distractions about us we see a recent issue of their energetic and practical minds. It has become a common joke that the only man who came out of the last war with any credit was Jesus of Nazareth.

Simple men and women everywhere are, to some of us, better than any great statesman ever expresses, even though they still look to him for guidance. Common folk are much more akin to the poet, who is, indeed, their true spokesman. There is more in Hardy's work of what soldiers have felt and said of war than in all the speeches ever made by politicians, from Pitt to the last of the famous leaders in war. Hardy the poet is ourselves, at our best. If there is a God to be known, it is by looking to such a man. If the word is ever made manifest in the flesh, and a purpose is ever made plain in the chaos of time and chance, there we have some clue to it. When the poet is crucified, then the multitude crucifies itself: the Pro-Consul's guard may march back to the palace satisfied that the road is cleared of the rabble. The poet is not a man apart, without aid for us in the manifold affairs of this busy world, an ineffective dreamer whose vision is unrelated to the things about us, and whose music is but Æolian and of the empty air. He is the best that the crude realities have created. He is the outcome of all our doubts and strivings. He, if we but knew it, is the true culture and the crowning flower of the mud and compost out of which he and all of us came. He, more than any other man, expresses what is the essential nature of the clay, and what it could be, and perhaps shall be.

XXX